CW00455558

C

By the same author

C

Peter Reading

Secker & Warburg
London

First published in England 1984 by
Martin Secker & Warburg Limited
54 Poland Street, London W1V 3DF

Copyright © Peter Reading 1984

British Library Cataloguing in Publication Data

Reading, Peter
   C.
   I. Title
   821'.914   PR6068.E27

ISBN 0-436-40984-4

SUBSIDISED BY THE
Arts Council
OF GREAT BRITAIN

Printed in Great Britain by
Redwood Burn Limited
Trowbridge

Acknowledgements

Some of this material has appeared in *Poetry Review* and *The Times Literary Supplement.*

(Incongruously I plan
100 100-word units.)

The brass plate polished wordless. Stone steps hollowed by the frightened hopeful ascending, the terrified despairing descending. (Probably between three and four months, perhaps one hundred days.) Out of the surgeries in this Georgian street, and similar streets in similar cities, some of us issue daily, bearing the ghastly prognostications. How we hate you, busy, ordinary, undying — taxi-driver, purveyor of the *Evening Star*, secretary bouncing puddings of malleable flesh. Incongruously I plan 100 100-word units. What do you expect me to do — break into bloody haiku?

> Verse is for healthy
> arty-farties. The dying
> and surgeons use prose.

*   *   *

The *Whale* is situated on the quay and is used by ferrymen and travellers calling for a quick drink before crossing. The *Colliers* is frequented by men from the pit. The fellow known as Tucker regularly attends both establishments. Perhaps he is in charge of the turnstile, the palm of his hand constantly grey from receiving pennies. Or he may be a gypsy, for he deals, apparently, in horses. He addressed me one evening in the bar of the *Whale* with importunate familiarity, remarking that I might henceforward know him as 'Char' (short for 'Charlie'?) or 'Mort' (short for 'Mortimer'?).

*   *   *

McGill-Melzack Pain Questionnaire word descriptors for scoring
methods:

Flickering, Quivering, Pulsing, Throbbing, Beating, Pounding,
Jumping, Flashing, Shooting, Pricking, Boring, Drilling, Stabbing.
Lancinating, Sharp, Cutting, Lacerating, Pinching, Pressing,
Gnawing, Cramping, Crushing, Tugging, Pulling, Wrenching,
Hot, Burning, Scalding, Searing, Tingling, Itchy, Smarting,
Stinging, Dull, Sore, Hurting, Aching, Heavy, Tender, Taut,
Rasping, Splitting, Tiring, Exhausting, Sickening, Suffocating,
Fearful, Frightful, Terrifying, Punishing, Gruelling, Cruel,
Vicious, Killing, Wretched, Blinding, Annoying, Troublesome,
Miserable, Intense, Unbearable, Spreading, Radiating, Penetrating,
Piercing, Tight, Numb, Drawing, Squeezing, Tearing, Cool, Cold,
Freezing, Nagging, Nauseating, Agonizing, Dreadful, Torturing.

Present Pain Intensity (PPI) intensity scale:

No Pain, Mild, Discomforting, Distressing, Horrible, Excruciating.

* * *

Disseminated spinal carcinoma.
I have lost all control and movement of
the abdomen, legs, feet and back. The growth
(particularly painful) on the spine
prevents my lying on my back. Bedsores
daily increase in size, restrict still more
manipulation of me on the bed —
nurses change my position every hour.
The open bedsores suppurate and stink . . .
I am abusive to a social worker.

We, trained Caregivers, can identify
symptoms like this — he is withdrawn and craves
attentive sympathy. Each afternoon
I persist — my ability to bear
his poor responses helps him to contain
his desperation. So there is much comfort.

* * *

When I was a boy and read that section at the end of Book V where shipwrecked Laertides crawls under two close-growing olives, one wild one cultivated, exhausted and finds shelter, I was deeply and permanently influenced. Since then the idea of such a comforting and comfortable solitary and impregnable bower has been inseparable for me from the concept of profound sweet sleep — and more . . . Almost every night since that time, except when drunken or erotic diversion has rendered such conceit impracticable, I have snuggled into the warm bedlinen metamorphosing it to dry Sabaean insulating leaves, blanding approaching oblivion.

* * *

[He breaks down and sobs embarrassingly.] The helpless things people scream out so childishly helplessly like 'Oh please I don't want to die I don't want to die I don't *want* to die!' Well, I scream them now I DON'T *WANT* TO   OH HELP ME PLEASE I DON'T *WANT* TO DIE I. [Drivel.] Why write it? Why ever wrote any of it? Poetry all weak lies, games. Epicurus, stupid lies, that there is nothing terrible in not living. Just to stay oh living, oh, why can't I? Stupid childish helpless poor little frightened [Pusillanimous drivel.] frail poor me. Us *all*.

* * *

Verse unvindicable; therefore sublate *The Ballad of Tucker's Tale*
(It's once he was a welterweight/And mingled with the champs/
But now he isn't fit, they say,/To make arse-holes for tramps —/
Kips in the Council's GRIT FOR ROADS/Fibreglass yellow bin/
And Tucker's Tale's known from the *Whale*/To the *Canny
Colliers Inn* . . .). During the war, Tucker's squad, randy in
France, was queuing up to shag a goat. A lance-corp jumped the
queue. Everyone complained, but, while the offender was on
the job, his head split suddenly apart leaking grey and crimson.
Sniper. Vita brevis; ars ditto.

* * *

Twenty of them. Should be sufficient. Comforting rattle from
the brown plastic bottle. Twist of cotton wool. Label typed
ONLY AS DIRECTED. Wrapped in linen in the rucksack: the
decanter engraved with my initials, the eighteenth century twist-
stemmed glass, the last bottle of 1894 Bual. Yapsel Bank, Hanging
Brink, Ashes Hollow, Grindle Nills, Long Synalds. A good
enough place to go stiff in. Quite unattended now, on hills
where once my sweet wife, my dear daughter . . . (enough of
that shite). Oakleymill Waterfall. Skewered by evening sun.
Fat, buttery fumosity of amber decanted Madeira. Sour chalki-
ness of the twentieth pillule.

* * *

I used to pepper my poetics with sophisticated allusions to *dear*
Opera and *divine* Art (one was constantly reminded of A. du C.
Dubreuil's libretto for Piccinni's *Iphigenia in Tauris;* one was
constantly reminded of Niccolò di Bartolomeo da Foggia's bust
of a crowned woman, doubtless an allegory of the Church, from
the pulpit of Ravello cathedral, ca. 1272) but suddenly these are
hopelessly inadequate. Where is the European cultural significance of tubes stuck up the nose, into the veins, up the arse?
A tube is stuck up my prick, and a bladder carcinoma diagnosed.
One does *not* recall Piccinni.

* * *

My husband never once entertained the notion of transcendent-
alism. He regarded it as an arrogant ('arrogant humility' is a
phrase he used of Buddhism, Christianity &c.), Quaternary,
Hominid invention for crudely pacifying the purely physiolo-
gical characteristic of Hominid cephalic capacity. He viewed the
concept of theism as cowardly, conceited, unimaginative and,
necessarily, at the *earliest* merely Pliocene. (His period was
Precambrian, before god.)

His irascibility increased towards the end . . .

[Missionaries visited him clutching 'Good News' bibles.] You are
importunate. Return to your corrugated-iron chapels and crave
forgiveness of your wretched deity for disturbing the lucubra-
tions of a bad hat.

* * *

It is a most terrible *bore*
to haemorrhage, spewing-up gore,
and, bubbling for breath,
be blood-drowned to death.
Je *ne* voudrais *pas* être mort.

You find the Limerick inapposite? Care for a cutely-adapted Adonic?

After he spewed-up
he was unconscious
till about tea-time,
when he woke up, then
vomited once more
(blood and fish-smelling
purplish matter).
Then he said 'Darling,
please do not leave me,
I think I'm —' nothing
else. He slumped heavy,
staining my clothing
puce and burnt-umber
(drying black later).
He was my husband —
we had been married
25 good years.

* * *

In ornithological days, at the observatory, we used, not in-
frequently, to discover moribund specimens. They seemed
always to have grovelled into some niche to quietly get on with
it — the stance would so often be trembling on a single weak leg,
the lids half-closed, the grey nictitating membrane half-drawn
across the, by then, dull bead. Several species, on dissection,
revealed carcinomatic infestation.

The use of narcotics, dehydration and breathing through the mouth have led to his mouth becoming troublesome. We prepare, in our pharmacy, an artificial saliva containing methyl-cellulose and glycerin which eases thirst and dry mouth.

* * *

[His wife and daughter tend him at home, bewildered by this revelation of his, of *all*, frailty. Special Laundry Services deal with his sheets and blankets — the soiling too foul for acceptance by normal laundries. The ambulance's arrival would be as the tumbrel's.]

Briskly efficiently deftly my daughter enters at midnight, eases me onto my side, changes the oxygen flask.

Even formed properly, no elegiac distich can fall with quite this sospirity: breath — out of a black mask exhaled.

None of it matters except at a purely personal level: pain, not oblivion, hurts; as with me, so with all quarks.

* * *

The specialist's hands, extremely large, buff-coloured, gently manipulate my emaciated wrist, two slender bones and a knot of turquoise vein. Huge tawny thumb and forefinger tighten on a frail pulse.

It was a good ferret and almost immediately there was a rabbit in the net. The man I was with (a gyppo-looking type whose company I cultivated as a child but whose name evades me now) removed it from the nylon mesh. His hands were huge and tawny and took up the rabbit, smoothing its ruffled fur, and with soothing fondness, with infinite gentleness, affectionately snapped its neck.

* * *

'His questions were probably mere pleas for reassurance. I did not tell him. I seldom tell them. Some of my colleagues disagree; many are of the same opinion as myself. According to Oken ("What to tell cancer patients", *Journal of the American Medical Association,* 1961, *175,* p 1120), about 80% of us rarely, if ever, tell them.'

According to Gilbertsen and Wangensteen ('Should the doctor tell the patient the disease is cancer?', in *The Physician and the Total Care of the Cancer Patient,* American Cancer Society, New York, 1961), about 80% of patients say they would like to be told.

* * *

His irascibility increased towards the end . . .

I am told that I was rude to a folk-singer who 'writes his own material' (of the You'll-Always-Be-On-My-Mind-Girl/Nuclear-Holocaust-Is-An-Awful-Shame School). He had, at his own considerable expense, caused a record of his ghastly outpourings to be manufactured. He solicited me to buy one. I declined. 'Why?' 'Because I believe you to be devoid of talent, mawkish and platitudinous.' (Sniffily) 'I'm not going to stay here and be insulted.' He went. It was as if one had flicked a smut from one's lapel.

* * *

'Quite the most maudlin man I've ever met
told me this in the lounge of the *Colliers*:
"It's many years ago now but, oh God!,
I can still feel her hand rubbing my tool
as she drove slowly down the pleached-hedged lane.
She stopped the car, licked her lips, moaned, and kissed me —
Christ!, slurping tongues like squirming warm oiled slugs —
and said 'God!, I could eat you' and unzipped
my washed-out Levi's, peeled them apart and guzzled.
I'll never see her again — I've got bowel cancer." '
Run them together, set as justified prose,
the inadequately blank pentameters.

* * *

Now for a bit of a trip down Memory Lane. Spring breakfast,
bluebells on sun-dappled gingham. A blue-hooped jug of cream,
bronzed toast, Frank Cooper's. Smoked aromatic crepitating
rashers. FREE!!! IN EACH PACK OF *BRAN-BREK* — A
PLASTIC BUG!!! I am served a dusty handful, read the packet.
Medical Scientists are in agreement. We all need fibre, and bran
is full of fibre. BRAN-BREK is full of bran, so eat BRAN-BREK.
Doctors say fibreless diets cause bowel cancer. Don't take the
risk — get into the BRAN-BREK habit. What was then fear has
become shitless terror.

* * *

Have you ever been in one of them? They really are depressing. Anyway, we were visiting someone — actually, the husband's mother it was, and the kid was with us so it all rather comes home to you that in a few years that'll be *you* in that bed and the kid, grown up, with *its* kid, visiting *you* . . . Anyway, in the next bed was this, you can only call it 'thing', — no bedclothes, just an official nightdress thing — and while we were telling lies to *our* one, *it* started up a sort of whining gurgling wheezing noise. [**To be continued.**]

* * *

[**Contd.**] I tried to crack on I hadn't noticed anything, but it kept on and on and I saw it was trying to attract my attention so I couldn't do anything but try to savvy what it was on about. It couldn't move, except sort of rock its head and flap one arm against its side. And all the time that queer noise. Its mouth wouldn't close and whenever it made that noise 'Waahg waah-grrglz' spittle with streaks of red dribbled out. It turned out that it wanted the screens pulled round it, and *I* had to do it. *Uuuugh!*

* * *

I seen him once before, before — you know. I was fetching a white Welsh, 12 hands, down Grindle Nills. Between Grindle Hollow and Oakleymill there was him and his Mrs and nipper. Picnicking, they was, wine cooling in the brook. He gawped at the nag's pricked ears, large eye, dished profile, withers, mane, poll, forelock, muzzle, chin, cheek, shoulder, chest, forearm, knee, cannon, pastern, chestnut, brisket, elbow, belly, stifle, gaskin, coronet, wall of hoof, heel, fetlock, hock, thigh, buttock, dock, croup, loins, back. He knew who I was alright. 'That's a pale one ye have there, Mr Tucker' he said.

* * *

At the end of the Cambrian, an estimated 52% of faunal families became extinct. At the end of the Devonian, 30%. At the end of the Permian, 50%. At the end of the Triassic, 35%. At the end of the Cretacious, 26%. Last night I had to get up frequently and stagger to the bathroom at the end of the ward. Pain unendurable. Rocked back and forth on lavatory seat, groaning. At the end of the Holocene (fashionable Tropical Rain Forest reduction, fashionable Nuclear Holocaust) the percentage of faunal family extinction is likely to at least compare with Cambrian figures.

* * *

[He writes] *Dear* [names of his wife and child which I render 'A' and 'B' for reasons of delicacy], *I recall our Callow Hollow alfresco. Our tiny child bathing in Oakleymill Waterfall pool. A gorse sprig suspended in an eddy. We were at the best of our lives. Such happiness never recurs. Never. Golden bright little flower, sharp thorns. Spätlese cooling in the gelid spring. Later, the gipsy with that pale gelding. I will remember these things until the day I die.* [Which is the day after tomorrow. He signs his name which I render 'C' for reasons of delicacy.]

* * *

'Retention can give rise to undue pain;/incontinence, conversely, causes shame/and a degree of inconvenience./ Colostomies, short-circuiting the bowel/to open on the frontal abdomen,/can cause distress at first, but nothing like/the anguish that the blockage, not relieved,/would cause. Soon after surgery, it seems,/some soiling from the new colostomy/is unavoidable — patients become/aware that they can get unclean and smell . . .'

Terminal verse. Rain-pits 700000000 years old in Precambrian rock: a species evolved 696000000 years after that: a handful of stresses and punctuation: ars only as long as vita: pentameters, like colons, inadequate.

* * *

100 days after diagnosis, I ingest soporifics. I compose octave and first line of sestet concerning my cadaver.

> The vagrant Tucker found it, partly rotted,
> Eyes gouged by corvids, puffed blue meat, wet, stinking,
> Blown lips serrated (nibbled as if pinking-
> Shears had been at them), maggoty nose besnotted.
> From its arse pocket he took five green-spotted
> (With penicillia) £5 notes — thinking,
> Quite rightly, they'd be better used for drinking
> Bass in *The Whale* than festering, rank, clotted
>
> In [something something something] Ashes Hollow

Why? Snot, gore, filth, suppuration of the arse-gut — for these *no* metric is vindicable.

* * *

A regular at the *Colliers* was Head of Art at the local Poly (phoney smoothie, used to take snuff). Mort bought some Itchy Powder from the *Wizard's Den* Joke Shop and one evening, when the Art bloke offered the old silver snuff-box round the bar, our hero slipped the irritant in (looked just like snuff) and handed back the antique. The offensive educationalist took no more stimulant until, on the motorway, driving back home, he indulged, and, in the paroxysm of sneezing that ensued, collided with an oncoming articulated lorry hauling meat-and-bone-meal and was killed instantly.

* * *

In the Borough Library the medical dictionaries are mostly used by unfortunates looking up their maladies. The Cs are particularly well-thumbed. CARCINAEMIA CARCINECTOMY CARCINEL-COSIS CARCINOGEN CARCINOGENESIS CARCINOGENIC CARCINOGENICITY CARCINOID CARCINOLOGY CARCIN-OLYSIN CARCINOLYSIS CARCINOLYTIC CARCINOMA-TOID CARCINOMATOPHOBIA CARCINOMATOSIS CARCIN-OMATOUS CARCINOMECTOMY CARCINOMELCOSIS CAR-CINOPHILIA CARCINOPHILIC CARCINOPHOBIA CARCINO-SARCOMA CARCINOSECTOMY CARCINOSIS CARCINO-STATIC CARCINOUS. I am researching C. ventriculi; the woman who has just relinquished Stedman's has marked faintly in pencil C. of uterine cervix. We are beyond verse here. No one wants to write 'On Last Looking Into Stedman's Carcinoma'. Neverthe-less, I have invented the 13-line sonnet for unlucky people (100 words, inc. title) . . .

* * *

Talking Shop

The three sterilizations went OK,
except for the advanced C. uterine cervix
(just my damned luck to find that) — anyway,
apart from that it all went normally.
The one in Number 2 was staggered when
I said 'We found your coil, by the way —
worked its way through the womb into the space
between the womb and stomach.' Number 3
(non compos mentis, got eight kids already)
asked me when 'it' would be alright again.
I said 'If you endeavour to avoid
sexual intercourse for about two nights . . .'
She said 'He won't wait. He *will* have his rights.'

* * *

His irascibility increased towards the end . . .

    The sham the twee and the precious/phoney-rustic ignorant/ wield their sugary Biros/down in the safe Sticks/ensconced in the done-up Old Wheelwright's./Poetical mawkish duff gen/ where a buzzard is 'noble' and lands/in a tree (surprise, surprise!)/ to corroborate some trite tenet/cum badly-observed Nature Note./ Their fauna is furry or feathery/people like you and me,/ cute or nasty — a raptor/becomes a Belfast terrorist./Bull-shit bull-shit bull-shit/of the Plashy Fen School./Peterson, Mountfort & Hollom/write more sense than you/bloody carpetbaggers.

*   *   *

According to Parkes ('Bereavement and mental illness', *British Journal of Medical Psychology,* 1965, *38*, p 1), 8% of seriously distressed bereaved people questioned expressed anger towards the dead person.

'She didn't seem particularly distraught. We were just with her at the ceremony. Suddenly she just seemed to ignore us all. "Why have you left me, why have you gone away? Why have you left me, why have you gone away? Why have you left me, why have you gone away? Why have you left me, why have you gone away?" She yelled and yelled as it went into the furnace.'

*   *   *

Muse! Sing *Phylloscopus trochiloides!*/I know it is a strange thing to recall/out of a rag-bag of experience/(rather than, say, rude goings-on with girls/or that first fright of Death — lost in thick fog/and with the tide coming in rapidly/over the mud-flats in the river mouth . . .),/but, more than early childhood or first dick,/this vagrant (which I mist-netted in youth)/incongruously gladdens my last thoughts/(and, more incongruous still, in quatorzain)./The wing formula confirmed that it was Greenish/ (rather than Arctic) Warbler — longer first/and shorter second primary, of course.

*   *   *

We went to picnic up Calo Holow to have a picnic to a worto-fall and a pool the pool was very deep. I neely fell into the pool. it was very suney We had cold chicin. Daddy and Mummy lay in the gras by the streem and I played round about and had oranj juse then Mummy and daddy had some wine that was cooling in the streem. Here is a powim of it

> When I went up Calo Hill
> I took some orang I did not spill.

> we saw a pale grey poniy
> Daddy fel asleep by the streem

*   *   *

It's bad for us as well, you know, looking after them. Can you take any more? I can't. I'm ready to give up. What's the use? All our patients die eventually. They should do six things for their 'Death Work': (1) become aware of their impending death, (2) balance hope and fear throughout the crisis, (3) *reverse* physical survival instincts, (4) relinquish independence, (5) detach themselves from former experiences and (6) prepare 'spiritually' for death. They go through six emotional states (outlined by Kübler-Ross): (1) Denial, (2) Isolation, (3) Anger, (4) Bargaining, (5) Depression, (6) Acceptance. All, eventually. All.

* * *

These are the sorts of things they say, through six emotional states (outlined by Kübler-Ross), sad, self-deceiving till the last ones: 'It's just one of those things' 'I shall be out of here soon' 'I'm getting better' 'I'm feeling fine' 'It's not so bad' 'I just need a good tonic' 'Be back at work before you can say "Jack Robinson" ' 'My pneumonia's worse than my cancer'. Can you take any more? I can't. I'm ready to give up. What's the use? All our patients die eventually. Anyway, those are the things they first say, DENIAL. Next comes ISOLATION:

* * *

'You don't know how it feels' 'You can't know how it feels' 'No one understands' 'They don't tell you anything' 'I try to guess what's going on' 'On your morning rounds you seem too busy to talk' 'No one seems to realize how vital my supply of oxygen is' 'I try to hide my feelings so that the family's not too distressed' 'Don't like being on my own' 'I don't like being left alone'. Those who we have not told start to sense it — the way the nurses look at them, the way we see less and less of them ...

* * *

Next comes ANGER: 'Why *me?*' 'They don't care' 'It's *my* body — they treat you like a child of 3' 'The food's lousy' 'The Quack's no good' 'A God of Love — huh!' 'The nurses is lazy' 'Why don't this happen to the scroungers and layabouts?' 'Doctor's a fool if he thinks this treatment will work'. Next comes BARGAINING: 'If only I could be home for the daughter's wedding, I'd not care after that' 'If only I could go without pain, I wouldn't mind so much' 'If only God would spare me to do His work a little longer, wouldn't mind then'.

* * *

Can you take any more? I can't. I'm ready to give up. What's
the use? All our patients die eventually. By now they can no
longer depend on their bodies doing what, before they got ill,
they thought they would do in such an eventuality — neither
suicide, nor smart philosophizing. They can not conceive
beforehand what it will be like. Dying nobly? My sweet arse
hole. One of them wrote verse. Verse! Write verse about this:
a Left Inguinal Colostomy. Shit, blood, puke and a body no
longer dependable, metastases, dyspnoea. . . I shut my eyes but
weep under the lids.

* * *

The fifth emotional state (outlined by Kübler-Ross) is that
of DEPRESSION: 'What chance have I got?' 'Not long now'
'What's the use?' 'This cancer is the end of everything' 'I'm not
going to get better' 'I'm so useless now'. Last comes
ACCEPTANCE: 'Thank you for all you've done' 'Dying will be
a relief' 'I see things differently now' 'The wife will be so
terribly lost and lonely'. These are the sorts of things they say
through the six emotional states (outlined by Kübler-Ross),
sad, self-deceiving till the last ones. It's bad for us as well, you
know.

* * *

I ndian doctor examines
N ewly performed colotomy (is appalled).

3

T erminal case, brought into
H ere last night, won't
E ver return to Azalea Terrace.

2

S mall frightened old woman,
A fter anaesthetic, has dim
M emory of fainting in chip-shop (won't
E ver get out of here).

1

V ery smooth-looking
E xecutive-type in
R oad accident; surgeons
T ry to revive him, fail;
I n collision with lorry
C arrying meat-and-bone-meal.
A n elderly lady, supposed suicidal,
L oudly denies taking barbiturates.

G

C oke is shovelled
O nto the furnace by a
L oathsome old stoker who now
U nfolds the Sports Page,
M arks with an X some
N ag for the next Meeting.

B

Mort or *Char* (this latter pronounced 'chair' or 'care' in their infernal accents, though, presumably, merely short for Charlie) possesses many katabolic anecdotes. His erstwhile leman bestowed finger-nail and teeth impressions on the mantelpiece as her distemper flourished and the burden of pain induced gripping and biting the mahogany often for hours together in the full excruciating anguish of the paroxysm. The huge firm 18-year-old malleable boobs she had let him enjoy were defiled at 42 by surgeon's scalpel and radium treatment. This, rendered into catalectic tetrameters, might do for the *TLS* or other reputable literary periodical.

* * *

What were bronzed on Margate sands,
flopped about by trembling hands,
malleable, conical,
have become ironical.
What was cupped in palm and thumb
seres now under radium.
What was kneaded like warm dough
is where, now, malign cells grow.
What was fondled in a car
through white silk-smooth slippery bra
(Marks & Spencer, 38)
was plump cancer inchoate.

Truncation (catalexis): 'frequent in trochaic verse, where the line of complete trochaic feet tends to create monotony. The following trochaic lines exhibit t.: "Simple maiden, void of art,/Babbling out the very heart". . .' — *Princeton Encyclopedia of Poetry and Poetics* (ed. Preminger).

* * *

He speaks to me and doodles the disorder's initial letter with green Biro in his desk-diary. Croissant? Banana? Sickle blade? He is frightened of what I will ask. Some of them will not tell you, nor prescribe what you really need. Perhaps an accumulation from a bogus insomnia claim, then, after the magnum of '61 *Cheval Blanc*, end with the 19th century Bual before taking them. Stylish finish, with the fine initialled decanter. Green discharge smothers the hideous curve, enormous now, and a suppurating colon punctuates it. I can almost scent the *Cheval Blanc* as I think of it.

*   *   *

when she first found it feel this she said oh god it can't be can it lump probably nothing he said better just x-ray be on safe side swarming teeming oh god if could turn back calendar only a few pages she went bald radium god pain bald horrible years ago on the Med when she god they were magnificent huge golden tanned god bald like a skull hugest on the beach

> [Cold truncating surgeon's blade
> razes what was St Tropezed.

Tomorrow she will occupy the 2nd floor Infirmary bed where now a patient from Azalea Terrace is expiring.]

*   *   *

'The husband was driving. The wife, aged 23, was in the back seat. They were on the motorway. She had just been discharged from a mental institution. Without comment she took 20 barbiturates. Suddenly the young man became aware that she was comatose on the sheepskin cover. He observed the empty brown plastic phial. In panic he screeched into a Services Area and — ' 'Why had she tried to, you know?' 'Terrible fear of getting cancer, no reason to suspect it, just kept thinking she would.' (Great unvindicable idea: a 17-liner, 100-word, pentameter acrostic, first letters forming *CARCINOMATO-PHOBIA*.) 'Continue.'

* * *

'He carried her into the Ladies' Lavatory intending to make her puke up the offending drug. She could not be made to vomit. An elderly lady, unable to enter the lavatory because it was thus occupied, sat on a chair outside the cubicle. Frenzied, the young husband raced to telephone for an ambulance, leaving his spouse unconscious in the toilet. He dialled 999 on the Cafeteria phone. The Cafeteria Manageress forced him to consume three cups of hot sweet tea. Meanwhile, ambulancemen arrived, accused the seated elderly lady of ingesting barbiturates, and, despite her protestations, bore her away by stretcher.'

* * *

Constantly anticipating cancer/(*A*bdominal, lung, throat, breast, uterus,/*R*ectum, 'malevolent' or 'benign'), she went/ *C*rackers and was soon certifiable./*I*nside, the loopiest of all was the/*N*ut-doctor who prescribed barbiturates/'*O*nly as soporifics – one per night'./*M*onths passed, and she accumulated 20./*A*t length she was discharged. Her husband called/*T*o chauffeur her. 'Apparently depressed/*O*r meditative, otherwise OK,/*P*erhaps a change of scene?. . .' Motoring back,/ *H*opelessly fraught, she polished off the lot./*O*verdose verdict brought by coroner. . ./*B*loody fool ambulance-wallahs kidnapped some/*I*dle bystander (whom they thought looked ill)/*A*nd left the suicide slumped in the bogs.

* * *

Ubi sunt the blue-green algae of yesteryear that by photo-synthesis first oxygenated the atmosphere? In the black cherts of the Bulawayan Limestone Group dated at about three thousand one hundred million years old, in the stromatolitic sediments first noted by Macgregor, later corroborated by Schopf et al; that is where. *Ubi sunt* the good old rain-pits and ripple-marks so transiently formed about six hundred million years ago? Buried in the Late Precambrian Longmyndian matrices of this valley where I myself. . . What is 40 years here or there on the chronostratigraph? (They don't make them like that anymore.)

* * *

When I worked with Schopf, on the Bulawayan stromatolites, I took twelve specimens of the limestone, each having a maximum dimension of 15 cm and exhibiting one or more areas of iron-stained, crescentic laminations of weathered surfaces. The best of these exhibited seven areas of lamination on the external surfaces and I gently broke it along the planes of weakness perpendicular to the laminations, exposing five additional laminated areas. I photographed the broken fragments and prepared a plaster cast of each. Those laminates were 3100000000 years old; I am dying (Carcinoma ventriculi) but the Holocene is of scant importance.

* * *

Ubi sunt J. William Schopf, Dorothy Z. Oehler, Robert J. Horodyski and Keith A. Kvenvolden, whose 'Biogenicity and Significance of the Oldest Known Stromatolites' (Journal of Paleontology, V. 45, No. 3, p. 477-485) so inspired us? They are now one with the cold stromatolitic limestone and laminated carbonaceous cherts of the Huntsman Limestone Quarries near Turk Mine, 55 km north-north-east of Bulawayo; that is where. *Ubi sunt* God? and pusillanimous Nietzsche (who merely substituted Übermenschen)? Sedimented. *Ubi sunt* Übermenschen? and the Master of the 100 100-Word Units? Sedimented, sedimented. (They don't make them like that anymore.)

* * *

'They are angry with their own failing bodies. . . also apt to criticize and blame others. . . One such aggrieved. . . greatly troubled the nurses and doctors who cared for her. . . Often young nurses would leave her bedside to shed a few tears because their attempts to help her had been met by contemptuous dismissal. . . accusing those who were treating her of apathy inefficiency and callousness. . . a way of expressing her disappointment and bitterness. . . for herself and the life that seemed unfulfilled. . .' — John Hinton, *Dying*, (Penguin, 1967).

His irascibility increased towards the end. . .
'Piss off, Sky Pilot', I whisper in the Padre's ear.

* * *

Sky cerulean. Sheep-cropped moist short sprung bright green turf where I lie, face up, my head on a stone at the brook edge. Upstream a metre and downstream a metre, trickling sound registers in each ear, an alto tinkling, a basso gurgling, the upper notes resembling skylark song, the lower resembling bathwater unplugged, concurrently continuously varying. My bare arms warm in bright sun. My husband beside me, touches. Suddenly our young daughter hugs me, hugs me again. Gewürztraminer rocks in the cool current. Cold roasted partridges in a white linen towel. Late Autumn, but, something irrevocably ~~pleasant~~ has occurred.
        lovely

* * *

My ward, 1A, was called Harley Ward (after the famous street, I assume). On arrival I was led into a tiny office to fill in forms which included questions like 'Have you been living in the UK for more than 12 months?' and 'Have your mother and father been living in the UK for more than 12 months?' Then I was labelled: a plastic strap was snapped round my wrist and inside its waterproof sheath was my name and number and what I was in for — colotomy. This perhaps reduces the likelihood of some innocent part being removed by mistake.

*   *   *

(Not just me, but all of us in the same vertical column. I pass the same hopeless pyjamad cases in ghastly contraptions daily. In the snot-green corridors daily the covered trolleys are shunted. Daily the meat-waggons swing through the gates braying, pulsing blue light, their burdens already history scraped off the Tarmac. Daily and nightly the trolleys the trolleys the trolleys jingle like gently shaken tambourines as they hasten with cargoes of shiny stainless-steel kidney-shaped bowls and glinting clamps, needles and blades and forceps, acres of soft white lint to one or another and finally all.)

*   *   *

Then I was led to my bed and shown my locker. I was to undress, stow away my clothes and lie down. A nurse curtained me off from the others. She recorded my temperature and pulse, took my blood pressure and shaved me with an old razor across the stomach from the navel down, removing about an inch of pubic hair. Then I produced a urine sample in a bed pan. After that there was nothing to do until the anaesthetist was due to see me at 5 pm. I produced my *Times* which was stolen by a marauding nurse.

* * *

The doctor had told me but not him. One evening he was struggling with a pile of papers — administrative stuff, to do with the conference on Early Precambrian Stromatolite Morphology and Taxonomy — when he slumped into his seat, exhausted by the simple exertion. I touched his arm and said (I hear my voice and its slight echo from the sparsely furnished study as if it is played back to me on tape) 'Oh my darling, you should not trouble with anything unessential; you see, you are dying.' He simply replied 'I understand' and replaced the documents in the mahogany bureau.

* * *

Radio-2 blared over a loudspeaker system. There was a radio with earphones behind my bed, so I tried to tune in to something else. There was a dial which read RADIO-1 RADIO-2 RADIO-3 RADIO-4. I clicked the indicator around the dial through three-hundred-and-sixty degrees. Radio-2 was vigorously transmitted at every calibration on the instrument. A trolley was driven at me by a gentleman with dirty fingernails. This vehicle supported a large urn of grey tea and a material bearing the legend BRAN SPONGE, BY THE MAKERS OF BRAN-BREK. I declined.

* * *

(Not just me, but out there in the Pedestrianized Precincts. The filth gathers beyond clearance or control. In gales the crisp yellow newspapers soar above the high-rises and out to sea or lodge in electric wires or pile up against shop doors. New desolate sounds of Coke cans discarded tinkling rolling in windy streets over greasy flags, and cables slapped clacking against tin masts of yachts in deserted lidos. In Department Stores staff outnumber customers now. The Cosmetics assistants, painted like Archie Andrews, look frightened at scant trade. In Furnishings, Glassware, Heel-Bar, Carpeting . . . something irrevocably dying is happening.)

* * *

The anaesthetist arrived, tampered with my heart and lungs, felt all round the ribs and implored me to breathe deeply while he listened. My blood pressure was up. He seemed desirous I should sleep and prescribed a soporific. I should be given a pre-med injection in the thigh about 2 pm on Tuesday and about 3 pm be taken into the Recovery Room and injected in the back of the hand to 'knock me out completely'. He'd 'bring me round' again and I'd be trundled back to bed. Incongruously, he inspected my fingernails. No doubt he found them charming.

* * *

Newsflash, their women writhe unconsolable in the dirt of Ulster and the Holy Land. They are not actresses; that is how they really feel. How I feel also, my cancerous husband. Newsflash after newsflash, their women writhe unconsolable in the dirt of Ulster and the Holy Land. They are not actresses; that is how they really feel. How I feel also, my cancerous husband. Newsflash after newsflash after stinking newsflash, their women writhe unconsolable in the dirt of Ulster and the Holy Land. They are not actresses; that is how they really feel. How I feel also, my cancerous husband.

* * *

I was fed Health Authority Chicken Supreme and semolina and jam and made to watch television where a woman turned into a spider during the full-moon, hunted respectable citizens, injected them with poison, swathed them in web cocoons and carried them off to her Transylvanian silo. I was given Ovaltine and sleeping-draught and endured insomnia all night. On Tuesday I was given tea at 6 am. 'Have you "performed"?' 'What do you mean?' I was given a suppository and told to keep it in for 20 minutes. I got cramp up the arse and shat after 5 minutes.

* * *

(Not just me, but the public clocks in the cities are fucked-up — /the Building Society one, the one on the Bank,/the one on the Town Hall, the one at the Station, all stopped/at a hopeless time and, whereas when I was a child/they were constants to be relied on, now the resources/and requisite knowledge to fix them are gone. And this isn't/some crusty superannuated old Colonel/lamenting, saying 'Of course, it was all fields then. . .',/but me, as my cardio-whatsit ticks limply, observing/ the clocks all knackered, whereas they used not to be.)

* * *

I have invented
a brand new kind of sonnet
where the octave is
a tanka plus a haiku
and the sestet two haikus.
But is there, today,
one ghastly experience
that vindicates verse?

Outside the chip-shop
an ambulance's blue light
throbs at heartbeat rate.
Someone has dropped dead;
tidily weighed syllables
drip from the draped stiff.

Why *verse*? At PRIDE OF PLAICE, the chippy opposite the
Leisure Centre, a horrible old human is slouched with its head
cradled in the alarmed proprietor's arms. Nearby a beggar swigs
White Horse, grey abrasive palm like a parched tongue
anticipating small coin.

* * *

Char helped the Undertaker once. The passenger had lived alone
in a cottage with a couple of dogs. It sat rigid in an armchair,
sap-green translucent glaze over the cheekbones. Char smoothed
the back of his finger gently over the brow (the skin was un-
pliable, cool, waxen) then leered, and between thumb and
grimy palm grasped the yellow lardy chin and shook it with
hatred. The grey tongue lolled. One of the dogs, a trembling
whippet, mounted the cadaver's bare knee, ejaculating after
several minutes' rut. Char pocketed £25 from the mantelpiece,
lowered the stiff into its fibreglass vessel.

* * *

Breakfast at 8 am was toast and tea. This was to be my last food for 24 hours. At 11 am I had a Savlon bath. I was given a sachet of concentrated disinfectant to put in the water and told to immerse to the ears and wash the face in it. I was put in surgical robes of crisp white linen and a gauze cap and returned to bed. I waited thus absurdly for the anaesthetist. Radio-2 was statutory. The first injection was 'in the bottom to gently relax you'. I scrutinized the ceiling for signs of change.

* * *

When I worked with Schopf on the Huntsman Quarry stromatolites, we concluded that the Bulawayan deposit could be interpreted as placing a minimum age (ca 3100000000 yrs) on the origin of cyanophycean algae, of the filamentous habit, and of integrated biological communities of procaryotic micro-organisms presumably including producers (blue-green algae), reducers (aerobic and anaerobic bacteria) and consumers (bacteria, predatory by absorption). This interpretation was supported by the occurrence of filamentous and unicellular alga-like and bacterium-like microfossils in other Early Precambrian sediments. I am dying (Carcinoma ventriculi) but what is 40 years here or there on the chronostratigraph?

* * *

Everything became pellucid. I seemed on the brink of some
revelation or original idea. Then I ceased to focus and my
eye-lids felt heavy. I think I dozed because the time went
very quickly. A Romany-looking stretcher-bearer shuttled
to and fro. I couldn't establish what he did with his poles.
The stretchers were canvas. A trolley would come in. He
inserted his poles. A patient was eased into bed. The poles
were removed. I could not see what he did with the poles. I
became irascible. I wanted to demand of him 'Account for
your poles, sir!'.

* * *

I should have started my sabbatical
but now it is impossible. Six weeks
ago they took the part-time employee,
hired to replace me, into hospital,
opened him up and said he had three months
before he pegged out — cancerous guts. They fetched
some out, but found too much inside.

He keeps
a sort of journal, so they say, in which
he chronicles his death in the 3rd Person,
partly in prose, part verse, peculiar, hey?
He's only young-ish too. So that's the end
of my sabbatical — I'm pretty miffed
(nor, I suppose, is he too chuffed about it).

* * *

I helped myself onto the stretcher. I was wheeled through the double doors into a bathroom-green room. The anaesthetist slapped my hand to raise a vein. 'You'll feel a small prick and a little scratch. There. Now it should be beginning to take effect.' I tried to say yes but said yuriuree. 'You may be feeling a cold sensation.' Yurayuaresss. A masked nurse in green said 'Can you see me? Can you focus on my face?' I tried to say yes but couldn't. I tried to say wind but said wiznera ah. She raised my head and I farted.

*   *   *

No verse is |adequate.|| Most of us |in this ward
will not get |out again.|| This poor sod| next to me
will be dead |in a month.|| He is young, |has not been
married long, |is afraid ||(so am I, |so am I).
When his wife |visits him|| (every day, |every day)
he takes hold |of her sleeve, || clutches her |savagely
screaming 'Please, |get me well!|| Dear sweet God, |make me well!'
Quasi sham |tétramètre, || sub Corneille, |sub Racine,
is too grand, |is too weak, || for this slow |tragedy,
screaming 'Please, |get me well!|| Dear sweet God, |make me well!'

*   *   *

Wheeled back to bed. I try to lift my arms. Cannot. The Romany performs with his mysterious poles. I am told to get some sleep. Staff Nurse calls the stretcher-blankets 'cuddlies'. Throat rusk-dry. I am uncomfortable but unable to turn onto my side. Eventually I heave myself onto my side. . . At an unknown time tea is brought. I feel sick. They wash my face and hands. The rubber under the sheets makes me sweat. BRAN-BREK is proffered. The surgeon who performed it appears. A pleasant, worried Sikh. He is afraid of what I am going to ask.

* * *

(Not just me, but also, out there, the cities whose shit/surges into the sea in tsunamis,/and Shopping Precincts whose shit of canines and rolling/Coke tins and paper and fag-ends and polystyrene/chip-trays and plastic chip-forks rattle in bleak winds,/and those who wash least, breed most, to all of us, all,/a shoddy incontrovertible burial in shit./

This isn't some crusty Colonel (retired) lamenting/'Of course it was all fields then, you see, in those days. . .',/but me, mé, suppurating to death,/not just on my own but with us all, with us all.)

* * *

Ubi sunt Chaloner ALABASTER, Guido BACH, William
CADGE, William Otto Adolph Julius DANCKWERTS, His
Excellency Dr. Johannes Friedrich August von ESMARCH, His
Honour Judge William Wynne FFOULKES, Sydney GRUNDY,
Henry HOOK, Eugene Clutterbuck IMPEY, James JOICEY,
Nesbitt KIRCHHOFFER, Chih Chen LO FENG-LUH, Budgett
MEAKIN, Alfred Trubner NUTT, John Orlando Hercules
Norman OLIVER, Mrs PUDDICOMBE, Harry QUILTER,
Rt. Hon. Sir Horace RUMBOLD, John SPROT, Gaspard le
Marchant TUPPER, Emanual Maguire UNDERDOWN, Thomas
Henry Bourke VADE-WALPOLE, Edward Montagu Granville
Montagu Stuart Wortley Mackenzie WHARNCLIFFE, His
Honour Judge Lawford YATE-LEE, Guiseppe ZANARDELLI?
(In *Who Was Who 1897–1915,* that's where.)

* * *

Some of us benefit from a self-shielding shunning of awful
thoughts about dying and, worse, physical pain at the end.

Nevertheless we are conscious of being falsely deluding,
when we say jauntily 'Oh! I shall be out of here soon!'

Adequate realization of what is truly awaiting
does not prevent us from this: never admitting we *know.*

Even though sometimes I talk about this abdominal cancer,
my mental ease demands lies, comfort of make-believe games —

such as this one that I play now in distich, almost pretending
verse has validity. No. Verse is fuck-all use here, now.

* * *

The meat-waggon comes for another unfortunate. Borne out of Azalea Terrace, the disgusting old victim looks glum, stunned, stupid, no longer working properly. There is bright pink spit dribbling onto the clean black sleeve of an ambulance man who holds one end of a stainless steel wheelchair thing and cradles the nasty head. Cold metallic joints lock slickly. A disinfectant whiff. One-way window. Blue pulse. Sitting on a yellow fibre-glass road-grit bunker, the Mad Tramp pulls at a whisky bottle (White Horse) and guffaws a perfect pentameter:

Hă há | hă há | hă há | hă há | hă há.

* * *

Evolution (including mass faunal extinction, at the end of the Cambrian, Holocene &c.) is what happens — not what *should,* according to *sapiens* interpretations, happen.

It seems to be the greatest pain I've known in my life. Respiration fails because of it, sweat streams, I think (I *hope*) I'll faint under it. Members of hospital staff are conditioned to pay no heed to (nor administer sufficient analgesics for) such excruciation. I feel mental as well as physical strain and inadequacy.

None of it *matters* (except at a purely personal level). Pain, not oblivion, hurts. As with me, so with all quarks.

* * *

[He breaks down and sobs embarrassingly.] Oh! I shall miss you so. Why has it happened? Why has stuff inside me suddenly gone terribly wrong? I don't think I'm afraid of not *being* anymore but so terribly terribly frightened of not being *with you*. And the child; no more playing catch with that large red-and-blue-spotted plastic ball. Never. Anymore. She called it Mr Spotty. [Mawkish drivel.] I can't be brave tonight. Oh my darling, help me! Look after me! Can't be brave or consoled by philosophy or by po — would willingly never have written anything if *only*

* * *

He had just died and screens surrounded the bed but the porter had not had opportunity to remove the body. I arrived at Visiting Hour when all the nurses were busy and unable to intercept me. I went straight to the screened bed and, employing a funny voice (derived from Donald Duck) which we had developed during our years of marriage for times of particular playfulness, addressed the occupant through the plastic panel thus: 'Howsqush my dearsqush old drake thisqush eveningsqush?'. Visitors at adjacent beds regarded me patronizingly. Then I bobbed my head round the screen and confronted the shroud.

* * *

[He writes] *Darling* [names of wife and daughter] *won't last (too weak) till Visiting Hour. Hope you find this. Last notes. Biro on Kleenex, fitting medium terminal words. Oh! Oh weep for Adonais he is dead. C3: the lowest grade of physical fitness in Military Service. On the filthy window-ledge of this ward a foul cleg in a patina of grease and dust whizzes around and around and. The only way to cross the Acheron is on inflated egos. Sleep after toil, port after stormy seas, Ease after war, death after life does greatly please. Two last Spenserians?* [Pah.]

* * *

Interdenominational claptrap,
from the Infirmary Chaplains, helps a few
cowardly of us bear our deaths. The chap
whom they leucotomized conceives this true:
that his soul is eternal. Such a view,
wholly unsatisfactory for me,
is genuinely good — he won't pull through,
but hopes to die without finality
accepting their dud-specious immortality.

Other poltroons amongst us, though, are scared
not of not *being* any more, but just
of terminal agony, are unprepared
[3ll. of MS. lacking ....
....
....]
Still more of us fear pain *and* being dust,
and for us nothing can (nor god, nor soul,
nor analgesic, nor philosophy) console.

* * *

It started with his urinating blood. We looked at it in the lavatory pan and were terrified. He went to morning surgery. He had to go for tests. They found he had a bladder carcinoma, little mushroomy things — we saw a photo. They forced something into him through a tube stuck into his penis hole. After the op they kept the tube in for a long time. It caused him to have a hard-on all the time it was in. He was in pain. He had to have regular check-ups. It seemed clear for ages, but recurred, *massively*.

* * *

[He breaks down and sobs embarrassingly.] I keep thinking *if only*. Oh, help me! And I can't believe it — that I am really going to   It is as if I were just writing about someone else d — just as if it were yet another of the things about those poor *other* people that I write (*used to* write) about. Why am I writing about it? Can't be brave tonight. [Drivel.] Oh, my darling, if only I could stay here not go not go not die! [Drivel.] Oh, I shall miss you so [Drivel.] terribly! terribly! Oh my dear darl [&c.]

* * *

Of course I have read Beecher ('The measurement of pain', *Pharmacological Reviews,* 1957, *9,* p. 59) and know that these opium-derived analgesics exert their principal effect not on the original pain but on the psychological processing of that pain. At first the effect was to allay fear and induce calm, even ecstasy. But my increasing tolerance to large doses and my increasing need for the drug have led them to consider Pennybacker's idea ('Management of intractable pain', *Proceedings of the Royal Society of Medicine,* 1963, *56,* p. 191) of leucotomy, meddling with the thalamus or with the frontal lobe.

* * *

Now I envisage the lachrymose mourning of my wife who loved me, there is the clearing of drawers, folding of vacated clothes.

'Here is the T-shirt and here are the denims he wore in the summer, well, he was then, and robust. Here is the green and red shirt

worn, I remember, as we walked together last year on his birthday. Here are the shoes he last wore — still in the treads of one heel

dry worms of mud and dead bracken remain from that day on
    Long Synalds.'
Empty, amorphous and cold, blue tubes of Levi's. She weeps.

* * *

'They feel worthlessness and emptiness without the deceased. "Now I am nothing." "Feel empty inside." (Loss of self-esteem.) They wish to believe the deceased is not dead. Happy and sad memories of the deceased. Concern for the deceased's missing life-enjoyment. "I am here not deserving to be alive while he is dead, unable to enjoy this lovely day." (Guilt.) "It is a dream; he'll be back tomorrow." (Need to deny the loss.) "I've disposed of his clothing." (Demonstrates *either* ability to relinquish bond to the deceased *or* compulsion to rid themselves of the pain which that clothing evokes.)'

* * *

Here are some of the things you'll need if it takes place at home: bed-care utensil set (inc. denture cup, kidney basin, bed pan &c.), large sheet of plastic, rented wheelchair, box of flexible drinking-straws, one bag disposable bed pads (the incontinent will use considerably more), large size disposable diapers (several boxes), thermometer, one bottle ethyl alcohol, cotton balls, lubricant, commode, a great many spare under-sheets, six wash-cloths.

Each nostril must be cleaned with a twist of tissue or cotton wool. Eyelids should be swabbed with wool swabs and warm normal saline, especially in the morning.

* * *

Since I deal daily with the incurable
I am familiar with a number of
similar cases — irrespective of
their social background, their reaction to
terminal pain democratizes them.
Today I sat beside a dying Cockney
(detect a patronizing tone? — OK,
the living *ought* to patronize the dying):

> 'The wife was upset, as she's never seen
> me like this. So I said "We've all of us
> got to go, Girl, I've ad a decent life;
> it's im in the next bed as I feels sad for,
> e's only young — they ad to stop is pain
> by a-leucotomizing-of is brain." '

*   *   *

[He writes] *Dear* [names of the Managing Director and one of
the editors of his publishers], *I am irritated to learn that
I shall soon be dead. You will be irritated to learn that by
then I shall have completed a final book. This epistle constitutes
one of its 100 sections. I shall be dead by the time you receive
this typescript. Set it in the old way — in Tedious Acrimonious
roman and Poppa-Piccolino italic on hand-deckled ipecacuanha
leaf bound in reversed brushed papoose.* [He signs his name.]

PS. Seriously, though, my wife will deal with proof correction.

*   *   *

[*Ubi sunt* the beldam who collapsed in Pride of Plaice, the micropalaeontologist with C. ventriculi, the hag carried off by ambulance from Azalea Terrace, the loon barbiturate ingester, the Master of the 100 100-Word Units, the C3 sniper victim, the lady with C. uterine cervix, the lady with breast cancer, the gent with bladder ditto, Epicurus, the jet-set exec-looking Head of Fine Art (snuff sternutator), the leucotomized folk-singer (singin whack for my diddle), &c^n? All planted, at the time of going to press. Some feared oblivion; most feared pain. Poor frail dear frightened little vulnerable creatures.]

* * *

so long as we exist death
is not with us;
but when death comes,
then we do not exist.
The diseases of my bladder
and stomach are pursuing   [Pah.]
their course, lacking
nothing of their usual
severity; but against all
this is the joy in
my heart at the

I knew what I'd got, I'd
seen it in my notes,
looked it up in the
medical books, knew I
couldn't recover. Wanted
to talk about it with
the doc but he always
seemed too busy, or just
called it inflamation.
Oh love, don't go, stay;
hold my hand, *tight,* love

* * *

I have administered anti-emetics and stool softeners and allowed him to eat and drink. He seems free of pain and nausea but vomits periodically whilst remaining comfortable. He describes the sensation as being similar to defecating — relieving an uncomfortable fullness. I treat his ascites with the insertion of a LeVeen shunt. Unfortunately he has developed fungating growths and draining fistulae. Particularly troublesome are the fistulae in the perianal area originating from the urinary and intestinal tracts. I performed Turnbull's Diverting Loop Transverse Colostomy (see *Current Surgical Techniques,* Schering, 1978). Bloody oozing, odour and haemorrhage occur from his decubitus ulcers.

* * *

My fistulae ooze blood and stink,
I vomit puce spawn in the sink,
diarrhoea is exuded.
Do not be deluded:
mortality's worse than you think.

You find the Limerick inapposite? Try the pretty Choriamb?

Bed-sores without; swarm-cells within.
Rancified puke speckles my sheets.
Faeces spurt out quite uncontrolled
into my bed, foetid and warm.
Vomit of blood tasting of brass,
streaked with green veins, splatters my face.

In vomiting, the glottis closes, the soft palate rises and the abdominal muscles contract, expelling the stomach contents. In nausea, the stomach relaxes and there is reverse peristalsis in the duodenum.

* * *

The list goes on and on interminably. . .
Rectal Bleeding, Chemotherapy
('Oh, how I dread the fortnightly injection —
the pain of it *itself,* and after that
ill for a week from the after-effects.
Anger is what I feel at dying, *anger* —
why can't the dropouts and the drunks get This?
I've always led such a clean, simple life. . .'),
Mastectomy, Metastases, Dyspnoea. . .
the list goes on and on and on and on. . .
(Some die in agony of mind and body
described by Hospice staff 'Dehumanized'.)
'Grief Work', 'Death Work', smug 'Terminal Caregivers'. . .
    I close my eyes but weep under the lids.

*   *   *

Crystalline water I sipped a few moments ago is returned as
vomit of discoloured filth, swarm-juice of rank-cancered gut.

C is for cardiac illnesses also — nothing to envy:
someone in High Street drops dead, shoppers, embarrassed/
        thrilled, gawp.

I can now vomit with accuracy and certain discretion
into the steel kidney-bowl, hourly they clear the puked slime.

Someone, nocturnally, in the adjacent corridor, expires:
I hear a bloody great thud, then someone mutters 'Now, *lift*'.

I can no longer depend on my body doing my bidding:
ill bodies baulk at deep thoughts (of suicide and twee verse).

*   *   *

It is not as one can imagine beforehand. Dysgneusia (an altered sense of taste occasionally occurring in cases of advanced malignancy) prevents my savouring the cigar-box-spiciness, deep, round fruitiness of the brick-red luscious '61 *Cheval Blanc,* the fat, buttery, cooked, caramel-sweet-nuttiness of the 1894 Bual.

'He is a patient with dysgneusia and severe dysphagia and a fairly advanced tumour for whom adequate hydration and nutrition are maintained by frequent small feedings of liquids. The insertion of an intraluminal esophageal tube is considered helpful. The dysphagia is due to an obstruction in the esophagus and hypopharynx.'

* * *

An absorbent pad placed under the corner of the mouth at night will prevent dribbling causing wetness and discomfort. Ice may help stimulate muscle movement. Pass an ice cube from the corner of his mouth towards the ear, then dry the skin. It may help to wipe an ice cube round his lips, then dry them. (One of them had some movement in the eyelids and was able to blink Morse messages.) Phrase questions to receive very simple answers, e.g.: 'There is jelly and ice cream or egg custard — would you like jelly and ice cream?' Pyjamas should be absorbent.

* * *

Never had a husband. No one to care when it happened except Jesus. Pain. Radiotherapy. Terrible terrible pain. No one to care. Energy gone. Tired. So weak. Hair falling out. *Actually falling out!* Bald. Quite bald. The Good Book. Had to give me a wig, National Health — couldn't've afforded it myself. Always put my trust in the Lord. Never missed a Sunday. But now, somehow. . . Oh what will happen? Oh Gentle Jesus meek and mild oh Gentle Jesus help me *save* me Gentle Jesus the Good Book, *Revelation,* vi. 8. Of course Mr Tucker comes to help, a real help.

*   *   *

In Ashes Valley this evening I crawl under
    sheltering bushes
Joined at the same stock, so close together they
    let no light through them
And where no rain can pelt through their meshed roof, so
    knitted together
One with the other they grow. And I merge myself
    into the brown husks.
Weakly I rake together a litter from
    dry leaves that lie here
Deeply sufficient to succour two or
    three if they wanted
Warmth against Winter however malicious the
    elements' onslaughts.
Thus do I bury me closely with leaf-mould and
    wait for Athene's
Soft anaesthetic, benign soporific, ar-
    cane analgesic. . .

*   *   *

> *final lines of the sestet*
> *of the final Petrarchan.*
> *'Hollow' forms the first*
> *c. I require dcdee. 'Follow'*
> *could be the second c.*
>
> | | |
> |---|---|
> | . . .by a vagrant. | *No. Something more prosy* |
> | There was an empty | *for this job. The morphine,* |
> | bottle, and, oddly, | *the colostomy — fuck-all* |
> | a glass and decanter | *there to justify lyric/metre.* |
> | — rather posh ones. | *But some structure still?* |
> | There was no money. | *Why? Dignity? — bollocks.* |
> | Oh, yes, and this | |
> | page of note-pad. . . | *But some structure still,* |
> | | *incongruously. . .* |
> | | |
> | | *100 units each of 100 words.* |
> | | *How about that? Neat. One unit* |
> | | *per day for 100 final days* |

*   *   *

Precambrian sub-division *Longmyndian,* ca. 600 million yrs. old. An individual Holocene *H. sapiens* with terminal pathogen. The co-incidence of these two, thus: approaching oblivion (by ingestion of soporifics), *H. sap.* picks up, from scree in Ashes Hollow, a sample of rock imprinted with 600-million-year-old rain-pits. Suddenly, alas, the subtle grafting of a cdcdee Spenserian sestet onto an abbaabba Petrarchan octave does not matter. Vita b.; ars b. Nor does the Precambrian sub-division *Longmyndian,* ca. 600 million yrs. old, nor Holocene *H. sap* with terminal &c., nor the *conception* of its not mattering, nor

*   *   *

(The suicide is untrue. Bodily weakness prevents my moving from the bed. The dismay to my wife and child which suicide would occasion renders such a course untenable. They would interpret my self-destruction as failure on their part to nurse me properly. Conversely, the grief my daily decline causes them is difficult for me to bear. If I could only end the terrible work and unpleasantness I cause them. . . But bodily weakness prevents my moving from the bed. Shit gushes unbidden from the artificial anus on my abdomen. My wife patiently washes my faece-besmirched pyjamas, for *prosaic* love.)